Lebanese Arabic Phrasebook
Vol. 1

HIBA NAJEM

ISBN: 9953031215
ISBN-13: 978-9953-0-3121-7

LearnLebaneseArabic@gmail.com

DEDICATION

While living in Beirut, I have had the chance to meet a lot of foreigners who visit the country each for his/her own different reason. Many of them were struggling with the language, since the Fusha, which they had made a lot effort to learn, didn't seem to help. (The modern standard Arabic or Fusha is a very decent and eloquent language that unites, and is the official language of, all the Arab countries.) The reason for that struggle is that every Arab country has its own dialect that differs from Fusha.

If your destination is Lebanon, than I recommend this book in order to feel free and confidant talking with the locals.

For the love of my country, which is sometimes very hard to love but at the same time very hard to leave, I dedicate my book to my language and to everyone who is willing to learn it.

CONTENTS

PREFACE

Some of you might have purchased this book because you already know me through my Lebanese Arabic teaching videos on Youtube. This book could be considered as an accompanying workbook for the Youtube channel "hiibanajem", as well as an independent Lebanese Arabic phrasebook for new students. The channel consists of a number of videos in which I teach the Lebanese Arabic dialect. It has been around since January 2011, and at the time of writing this book, there are around 50 videos available for everyone to watch.

The purpose of this book is not only to organize all the material taught on the channel throughout the many lessons and to provide a written reference for the students who already have watched the videos, but also to offer new students a more structured access to the material where they could learn the dialect and use the videos as additional guides to deepen their understanding. The last section of this book will consist of language puzzles such as crosswords, word search and fill-in-the-blanks that will help you master the material.

1 INTRODUCTION

The method of teaching is vaguely inspired by the Rosetta Stone method that teaches the dialect through using practical sentences instead of memorizing strict grammatical rules.

All the words and phrases are transcribed from the videos, so there will be a reference to the relevant video below each sentence. You will be able to hear the correct pronunciation in order to master your accent and find detailed explanations of each word in complicated phrases.

The sentences will be divided into themes like "Introductions" or "Travelling" and they will be written in 3 forms:

1.   In English first.

2.   Then in Lebanese transliteration (Latin alphabet) for people who can't read Arabic.

3.   And eventually in Lebanese (Arabic alphabet) for those who are Arabic literate.

Transliteration Guidelines

Since the Arabic alphabet is quite different from the Latin one that does not include the same letters, we'll have to agree upon certain rules that we'll use throughout the book as to avoid any confusion. The representations chosen will be based on their simplicity in contrast with the academic but more complex symbols such as [ʔ] or (ħ). There will be a table presenting each letter and its transliterated representation, preceded by an explanation of some of the letters used. While the table might only be useful for Arabic readers, the explanation will help all readers to recognize the sounds of the transliteration. If any of the following information seems too complicated for you, don't worry, you will find it to be simpler as you go along and read the actual words and phrases. These are just guidelines you can refer to if you find any difficulty in reading transliterations:

1. The Hamza (ء) which is a glottal stop, is not a full letter and is not one of the 28 letters of the alphabet but it is widely used in the language and especially in the Lebanese dialect, as in most Lebanese areas, the Qaf (ق) (pronounced as a "K" or a "Q" in standard Arabic) is pronounced as a Hamza and labeled as a glottal stop. The Hamza is phonetically represented as /ʔ/ while academically represented as a "modifier letter right half ring" (ʼ) which will be replaced by an apostrophe in this book ('). You might find it to be represented with the number (2) on the web, as this is the conventional chatting representation of it, inspired by the inverted similarity in shape of the (2) and the (ء).

2. The Aleph (ا), the first letter of the Arabic alphabet, takes many forms, depending on its accentuation and on the placement of the Hamza in relation to it, facts that change the way it sounds. It might sound as a glottal stop or as a long vowel. For this reason, in cases where it sounds as a glottal stop it will be transliterated as a simple Hamza (ʾ) and in cases where it sounds like a vowel, it will be represented with the respective vowels (a), (e), (i), (o), or (ei). The latter, (ei), is used as the sound of the accentuated letter (é).

3. Thaa' (ث), is an Arabic letter that sounds like (th) in English words like (th)ink or ba(th), but in the Lebanese dialect it is most commonly replaced by either a (t) or an (s) sound. So it might be written in words as a (ث), but pronounced as is written in the Transliteration. (Ex: Snow=Talej= تلج)

4. The Arabic letter (ع) or Ayn has no similar letters or sounds in the Latin alphabet. It is articulated with the back of the throat and the root of the tongue. It is phonetically represented as /ʕ/, while its academic representation is the "modifier letter left half ring" (ʿ) which is similar to the representation of the Hamza. In order to avoid any confusion between the Hamza and the Ayn, the latter will be represented as it is in chatting forums with the number (3) because of its mirrored resemblance to (ع) "3ayn".

5. Ghayn (غ) is a variant of 3ayn (ع) in shape but is

different in sound. The closest popular equivalent to its sound is the Parisian French (r). It is phonetically represented as /ɣ/ but most commonly transliterated as (gh) which we will use throughout the book.

6. The Haa' (ح) which is similar to the 3ayn in articulation (with the back of the throat and the root of the tongue) but different in phonation is represented phonetically as /ħ/ and academically as (ḥ) while in this book it will be represented as a capital (H) which is usually the simplest symbol of the Haa'. You might find that it is sometimes written as a (7) because of the number's resemblance to the upper part of (ح).

7. The Khaa' (خ) is pronounced in a way that is very similar to German, Scottish, and Polish (ch), Russian (x), and Spanish (j). It is phonetically represented as /x/, while its most common transliteration is (kh) which is used almost everywhere and is therefore used in this book. You might also find it to be represented as (5) which also resembles a distorted mirrored (خ) missing the dot.

8. Thaal (ذ) and Thahh (ظ) which are variant of each other, and resemble the sound of the English (th) in (th)is or fea(th)er, is most commonly replaced by either a (d) or a (z). Ex: Memory=Zeikra= ذاكرة)

9. Finally, some words end with the sound (é), or might have this sound in the middle of the word. These will be transliterated as (eh) in the end, and

(ei) in the middle.

As for the Lebanese words written in the Arabic alphabet, words ending with the (a) sound in Lebanese will be written:

1. as (ا) whenever the same word in Modern Standard Arabic end with (اء) or (مَا) like حَمراء or عَندها, written as حَمرا or عَندا

2. as (ة) whenever the word is feminine and has a masculine version, like رايحة

3. otherwise, they will be seen as (ه)

The Arabic Letters and Their Transliteration According To the Lebanese Dialect

١	a | i | o | e | ei
ب	b
ت	t
ث	t | s
ج	j
ح	H
خ	kh
د	d
ذ	d | z
ر	r
ز	z
س	s
ش	sh
ص	s
ض	d
ط	t
ظ	d | z
ع	3
غ	gh
ف	f
ق	ʿ
ك	k
ل	l
م	m
ن	n
ه	h
و	w | ou
ي	i | y

The Chapters

There are seven chapters in this book. The first six define categories of the phrases taught throughout the chapters, while the last one is dedicated for language exercises and puzzles.

The first chapter entitled "Basic Language" contains five subcategories: Numbers, Colors, Days, Pronouns and Prepositions.

The second chapter, "Travelling", offers sentences that you will need if you are travelling to Lebanon and the subcategories are arranged by what you might chronologically use: Airport, Directions, Money, Accommodation and Shopping.

The third, fourth and fifth chapters will contain everyday sentences as well as phrases to use around friends, family and in relationships and conjugations of a few verbs that might be useful. They will also shed light on how conjugation works in the Lebanese Arabic dialect.

The sixth is the last chapter containing phrases. It will have a variation of random sentences, uncategorized, which I have been asked to teach by viewers of the videos or which I have found to be practical and fun to be learnt.

The final chapter, as mentioned above, will consist of "fill in the blank" exercises, as well as crosswords and word search puzzles. If you wish to print many copies of the puzzles, or probably wish to enlarge them, please sign up at the following link for a PDF version of the puzzles and their solutions: **http://bit.ly/ExercisesPDF** Just enter the link in the address bar of your internet browser and hit the Enter button.

2 CHAPTER 1: BASIC LANGUAGE

Numbers

Zero	صِفِر **sefer** *Video Lesson 4*
One	واحد **waHad** *Video Lesson 4*
Two	تنَين **tnein** *Video Lesson 4*
Three	تلاتِه **tleiteh** *Video Lesson 4*
Four	أربعَه **arb3a** *Video Lesson 4*

Five	خمسه **khamseh** *Video Lesson 4*
Six	ستّه **setteh** *Video Lesson 4*
Seven	سَبعَه **sab3a** *Video Lesson 4*
Eight	تمانه **tmeineh** *Video Lesson 4*
Nine	تسعه **tes3a** *Video Lesson 4*
Ten	عشره **3ashra** *Video Lesson 4*

Days

Monday	تَنين tanein Video Lesson 14
Tuesday	تَلاتَه taleita Video Lesson 14
Wednsday	أُربعا orb3a Video Lesson 14
Thursday	خَميس khamees Video Lesson 14
Friday	جمعه jem3a Video Lesson 14
Saturday	سَبت sabet Video Lesson 14
Sunday	أَحَد aHad Video Lesson 14

Today	اليَوم **lyom** <u>Video Lesson 7</u>
Today is Monday	اليوَم التَنَين **lyom el tanein** <u>Video Lesson 7</u>
Morning	صُبح **sobeH** <u>Video Lesson 7</u>
Noon	ضُهر **doher** <u>Video Lesson 7</u>
Night	لَيل **leil** <u>Video Lesson 7</u>
Moon	أمَر **amar** <u>Video Lesson 19</u>
Sun	شمَس **shames** <u>Video Lesson 21</u>
Autumn	خَريف **khareef** <u>Video Lesson 7</u>

Winter	شِتي sheteh Video Lesson 7
Spring	رَبيع rabee3 Video Lesson 7
Summer	صَيف|صَيفيه sayf | sayfiyeh Video Lesson 23
We are now in the spring	نِحنا هَلَّء بِفَصل الربيع neHna halla' b fasl el rabee3 Video Lesson 7
It's sunny but it's not very hot	في شَمَس ومِش كتير شوب fi shames w mesh kteer shob Video Lesson 7
In the summer we go to the beach	بالصَيف مِن روح عَلى البَحر bl seif mn rouH 3al baHer Video Lesson 7
The sun is setting	الشَمَس عَم بتغيب el shames 3am betgheeb Video Lesson 7

Colors

Red	حَمرا/ أَحمَر **Hamra/aHmar** Video Lesson 22
Green	خَضرا/ أَخضَر **khadra/akhdar** Video Lesson 22
Blue	زَرقا/ أزرق **zar'a/azra'** Video Lesson 22
Yellow	صَفرا/ أَصفَر **safra/asfar** Video Lesson 22
Black	سَودا/ أَسوَد **sawda/aswad** Video Lesson 22
White	بَيضا/ أَبيَض **bayda/abyad** Video Lesson 22
Grey	رمَادي **rmeideh** Video Lesson 22

Purple	بَنَفسَجي **banafsajeh** Video Lesson 22
Pink	زَهري **zahreh** Video Lesson 22
Brown	بنّي **benneh** Video Lesson 22
Red balloon	بَالون أَحمَر **balon aHmar** Video Lesson 'Valentine'
Red flower	ورdِه حَمرا **wardeh Hamra** Video Lesson 'Valentine'

Pronouns

I	أنا **ana** Video Lesson 13
You	إنتِ/إنتَ **enteh/enta** Video Lesson 13
He	هوّي **howeh** Video Lesson 13
She	هيّي **hiyeh** Video Lesson 13
We	نِحنا **neHna** Video Lesson 13
You (plural)	إنتو **ento** Video Lesson 13

They	هنّي
	henneh
	Video Lesson 13

Prepositions

And	وَ **wa** <u>Video Lesson 10</u>
So	فَ **fa** <u>Video Lesson 10</u>
But	بَس **bas** <u>Video Lesson 10</u>
To (location)	عَلى **3ala** <u>Video Lesson 10</u>
To (cause)	تَ **ta** <u>Video Lesson 10</u>
After	بعدين **ba3dein** <u>Video Lesson 10</u>

When	لمَّا lamma Video Lesson 10
From	مِن men Video Lesson 10
On	عَلى 3ala Video Lesson 10
About	عَن 3an Video Lesson 10
That	إنّو enno Video Lesson 10
Because	لأنّو la'enno Video Lesson 10

So finally we agreed on the red color	فَأخيرا" إتفأنا عَلى اللّون الأحمَر **fa akheeran ttafa'na 3ala el lon el aHmar** <u>Video Lesson 10</u>
I would like to come but I'm traveling	عَبالي إجي، بَس مسافرة/مسافَر **3abeileh ejeh, bas msefra/msefar** <u>Video Lesson 10</u>
She's going to the gym	هِيّي رايحة عَلى النادي **hiyeh rayHa 3al neideh** <u>Video Lesson 10</u>
Eat the sandwich then the chocolate	كول العروس بعدين الشوكولا **kol el 3arous ba3dein el chocola** <u>Video Lesson 10</u>
I will call you when I get back	بحكيك لمًا إرجَع **beHkeek lamma erja3** <u>Video Lesson 10</u>

I buy milk from the supermarket	أنا بشتري حَليب من السوبرماركت **ana beshtereh Halib men el supermarket** Video Lesson 10
My book is on the table	كتابي عَلى الطاوله **kteibeh 3ala el tawleh** Video Lesson 10
I'm talking about last night	عَم بحكي عَن مبارح **3am beHke 3an mberiH** Video Lesson 10
He said that he will come	هوّي آل إنّو جايي **howe 'aal enno jeyeh** Video Lesson 10
He said that she's coming	هوّي آل إنّا جايي **howeh 'aal enna jeyeh** Video Lesson 10

| I am here because I lost my baggage | أنا هون لأنّو ضَيَّعت غراضي\|شِنطي
ana hon la'enno dayya3et ghradeh \| shenateh
<u>Video Lesson 10</u> |

3 CHAPTER 2: TRAVELLING

Airport

Welcome to Lebanon	أهلا و سَهلا بلِبنان **ahla w sahla b lebnein** <u>Video Lesson 2</u>
Excuse me my baggage is late	عَفوا"، شِنَطي|غراضي تأخَرِت **3afwan, shenateh | ghradeh t'akharit** <u>Video Lesson 2</u>
Excuse me I lost my baggage	عَفوا"، ضَيَعت شِنَطي|غراضي **3afwan, dayya3et shenateh | ghradeh** <u>Video Lesson 2</u>

Excuse me I want to exchange money	عَفوا"، بَدّي صرَّف مَصَاري **3afwan, baddeh sarrif masareh** <u>Video Lesson 2</u>
Hello I want to go to Ashrafieh	مَرحَبا، بَدّي روح عَلى الأشرَفيّه **marHaba, baddeh rouH 3al Ashrafieh** <u>Video Lesson 2</u>

Directions

Where am I?	أنا وَين؟ ana wein? Video Lesson 5
Left	شمال shmeil Video Lesson 5
Right	يمين yameen Video Lesson 5
Straight	دِغري deghreh Video Lesson 5
Road	طريء taree' Video Lesson 5
Square	ساحَه seiHa Video Lesson 5

How to go to Hamra	كيف بروح عَلى الحمرا؟ **kif brouH 3al Hamra?** <u>Video Lesson 5</u>
What's the name of the street	شو إسم الشارِع؟ **shou esem el sheiri3?** <u>Video Lesson 5</u>
Which bus should I take?	أيّا باص باخد؟ **ayya bus beikhoud?** <u>Video Lesson 5</u>
Does the bus pass by here	بيأطع الباص مِن هون؟ **byo'ta3 el bus mn hon?** <u>Video Lesson 3.2</u>
Is there a restaurant nearby?	في مَطعَم أريب مِن هون؟ **fi mat3am areeb mn hon?** <u>Video Lesson 5</u>
Last question, is there a map	آخِر سوآل، في خريطه؟ **ekhir sou'aal, fi khareeta?** <u>Video Lesson 3.2</u>

Money

250	ميتَين و خَمسين **meetein w khamseen** Video Lesson 4
500	خَمس ميّه **khams miyyeh** Video Lesson 4
1000	ألف **alf** Video Lesson 4
5000	خمس–ة–آلاف **khams-t-aleif** Video Lesson 4
10000	عشر–ة–آلاف **3asher-t-aleif** Video Lesson 4
20000	عِشرين ألف **3eshreen alf** Video Lesson 4
50000	خَمسين ألف **khamseen alf** Video Lesson 4

100000	ميّة–ألف **meet alf** <u>Video Lesson 4</u>

Accommodation

Hello I want to reserve a room	مَرحبا بَدّي إحجُز أوضه **marHaba baddeh eHjouz ouda** Video Lesson 3.1
I'm looking for a small room with one bed	أنا عَم فَتِّش علي أوضة صغيرة مَع تخت واحَد **ana 3am fattish 3ala ouda zgheereh ma3 takhet waHad** Video Lesson 8
I want it for one week	بَدّي يَاها لجمعه **baddeh yeha la jem3a** Video Lesson 3.1
How much should I pay	أدّاي لازِم إدفَع؟ **addeh lezim edfa3?** Video Lesson 3.1
I want the cheapest room	بَدّي أرخَص أوضه **baddeh arkhas ouda** Video Lesson 3.1
What time is breakfast served	أيّا ساعه الترويقه؟ **ayya se3a el terwee'a?** Video Lesson 3.1

Home	بَيت beit Video Lesson 8
Apartment	شِأّه she'a Video Lesson 8
An apartment for rent	شِأّه للأجار she'a lal ajar Video Lesson 8
I'm looking for an apartment to rent	عَم فتِّش على شِأّه للأجار ana 3am fattish 3ala she'a lal ajar Video Lesson 8
Where can I find an apartment to rent	وين فيني لاقي شأّه للأجار؟ wein feeneh lei'eh she'a lal ajaar? Video Lesson 8
How much should I pay per month	أدّاي لازِم إدفَع بالشهر؟ addeh lezim edfa3 bel shaher? Video Lesson 8

30

Are the electricity and water bills included?	الكهرَبا والمَي ضُمن الأجار؟ el kahraba wel may domn el ajaar? Video Lesson 8
Is the bathroom common?	الحَمام مُشترَك؟ el Hemmeim moushtarak? Video Lesson 8

Shopping

Shirt	أميص **ameess** <u>Video Lesson 11</u>
High heels	سكربينِه **scarbeeneh** <u>Video Lesson 11</u>
Shoe	صُبَّاط **sobbat** <u>Video Lesson 11</u>
Dress	فُستان **fostan** <u>Video Lesson 11</u>
Glasses	عوينات **3wayneit** <u>Video Lesson 11</u>
How much does it cost	أدّاي حأّا/حأّو؟ **addeh Ha'a/Ha'o?** <u>Video Lesson 11</u>
How much do you want	أدّاي بِتريد؟ **addeh betreed?** <u>Video Lesson 2</u>

Is there another size	في غَير إياس؟ **fee gheir 'yeiss?** Video Lesson 11
I need a smaller one	بدّي إياس أَصغَر **baddeh 'yeiss asghar** Video Lesson 11
I need a larger one	بدّي إياس أَكبَر **baddeh 'yeiss akbar** Video Lesson 11
In how many colors does it come	كَم لون في مِنّا؟ **kam lon fi menna?** Video Lesson 11
Does it look good on me	حِلوة/ حِلو علَيّ؟ **Helweh/Helo 3layyeh?** Video Lesson 11
Are the items on sale	في "سايل"/عامِلين "سايل"؟ **fee sale? | 3amleen sale?** Video Lesson 11
Can I get it for a better price?	فيكي ترَخصيلي/فيك ترَخصلي؟ فيكي تعمليلي سِعر/فيك تعمِلّي سِعر؟ **feekeh trakhseeleh/feek** **trakhessleh? | feekeh** **ta3mleeleh/feek ta3melleh** **se3er?** Video Lesson 11

4 CHAPTER 3: EVERYDAY WORDS AND SENTENCES

Introductions

Hello how are you	مَرحبا كيفِك/كيفَك/ كيفكُن؟ marHaba keefik/keefak/keefkoun? <u>Video Lesson 1</u>
Good morning	صبَاح الخير إصبَاح النور sabaH el kheir|sabaH el nour <u>Video Lesson 9</u>
Good evening	مَسا الخَير إمَسا النور masa el kheir | masa el nour <u>Video Lesson 9</u>

How are you?	كيفِك/كيفَك/كيفكن keefik/keefak/keefkoun? Video Lesson 9
What's your name	شو إسمِك؟ إسمَك؟ shou esmik/esmak? Video Lesson 15
What do you work	شو بتشتغلي/بتشتغل/بتشتغلوا؟ shou bteshteghleh/bteshteghil/bteshteghlo? Video Lesson 15
I work as a translator	بِشتغل تِرجمان beshteghil terjmein Video Lesson 1
My name is Maria I come from Mexico to study Arabic	إسمي ماريا، جايي من المكسيك إدرُس عَربي esmeh Maria, jeyeh mnel mexeec edrous 3arabeh Video Lesson 1
What do you study	شو بتدرسي/بتدرُس/بتدرسوا؟ shou btedrseh/btedrous/btedrso? Video Lesson 15

What did you study	شو دَرَستي/دَرَست/درستوا؟ shou darasteh/daraset/darasto? <u>Video Lesson 15</u>
Where are you from	مِن وَين إنتِ/ إنتَ؟ min wein enteh/enta? <u>Video Lesson 15</u>
Where do you live	وَين آعدي/آعِد/آعدين ساكني/ساكِن/ساكنين | عايشي/عايش/عايشين؟| wein 'ei3deh/'ei3id/ei3deen | seikneh/seikin/seikneen | 3aaysheh/3aayish/3aayshee n ? <u>Video Lesson 15</u>
What do you do after work	شو بتَعملي/بتَعمِل/بتعملوا بعد شغلِك/شغلَك/شغلكن؟ shou bta3mleh/bta3mil/bta3mlo ba3ed sheghlik/sheghlak/sheghel koun? <u>Video Lesson 15</u>
Do you do sports	بتَعملي/بتَعمُل/بتعملوا رياضة؟ bta3mleh/bta3mil/bta3mlo sport? <u>Video Lesson 15</u>

36

What's your phone number	شو رأمِك/رأمك/رأمك/أرآمكن؟ **shou ra'mik/ra'mak/ar'aamkoun ?** <u>Video Lesson 15</u>
I'll call you maybe we'll go out someday	رَح إحكيكي/ إحكيك بَركي منَعمُل شي،شي نهار **raH eHkikeh/eHkik barke mna3mil shi, shi nhar** <u>Video Lesson 15</u>
What's new	شو في جديد؟ **shou fi jdeed?** <u>Video Lesson 9</u>
It was nice seeing you	مبَسَطِت شفتِك/شفتَك/ شِفتكُن **mbasatet sheftik/sheftak/sheftkoun** <u>Video Lesson 9</u>

General

What do you want?	شو بدِّك/ بدّك/ بدكُن **shou baddik/baddak/baddkoun?** <u>Video Lesson 6</u>
Do you want something?	بدِّك/بدّك/بدكُن شي؟ **baddik/baddak/badkoun shi?** <u>Video Lesson 6</u>
Can you help me	فيكي تساعديني؟/فيك تساعدني؟/فيكُن تساعدوني؟ **feekeh tse3deeneh/feek tse3edneh/feekoun tse3douneh?** <u>Video Lesson 11</u>
What happened?	شو صار؟ **shou sar?** <u>Video Lesson 9</u>
What's happening?	شو عم بصير؟ شو في؟ **shou 3am b seer? Shou fi?** <u>Video Lesson 9</u>
How was your day?	كيف كان نهارك/ نهارَك/نهاركُن؟ **keef kein nharik/nharak/nharkoun?** <u>Video Lesson 9</u>

What are you doing tomorrow	شو عاملي/ عامِل/عاملين بُكرا؟ shou 3aamleh/3aamil/3aamleen bukra? Video Lesson 9
I will see you soon	بشوفِك/بشوفَك/بشوفكن أريباً bshoufik/bshoufak/bshoufk oun areeban Video Lesson 9
I will call you	بحكيكي/ بحكيك/ بحكيكُن beHkeekeh/beHkeek/beHk eekoun Video Lesson 9
My friend and I are studying	أنا ورفيئتي/ رفيئي عم نِدرُس ana w rfee'teh/rfee'eh 3am nedrous Video Lesson 10

Greetings

Merry Christmas	ميلاد مَجيد **mileid majeed** Video Lesson 17
Happy new year	عام سَعيد **3aam sa3eed** Video Lesson 17

CHAPTER 4: FAMILY, FRIENDS AND
RELATIONSHIPS

Family

Family	عَيلَه **3ayleh** Video Lesson 12
Father	بَيِّي **bayyeh** Video Lesson 12
Mother	إمِّي **emmeh** Video Lesson 12
Brother	خَيِّي **khayyeh** Video Lesson 12

Sister	إختي ekhteh Video Lesson 12
Grand-mother	سِتِّي setteh Video Lesson 12
Grand-father	جدّي jeddeh Video Lesson 12
Aunt (paternal)	عَمتي 3ammteh Video Lesson 12
Aunt (maternal)	خَالتي khalteh Video Lesson 12
Uncle (paternal)	عَمّي 3ammeh Video Lesson 12
Uncle (maternal)	خَالي khaleh Video Lesson 12

Cousin (female)	بِنت خالتي/خالي/عَمتي/عَمِّي bent khalteh/khaleh/3ammteh/3ammeh Video Lesson 12
Cousin (male)	إبن خالتي/خالي/عَمتي/عَمِّي eben khalteh/khaleh/3ammteh/3ammeh Video Lesson 12
Husband	جَوزي jawzeh Video Lesson 12
Wife	مَرتي marteh Video Lesson 12
Daughter	بِنتي benteh Video Lesson 12
Son	إبني ebneh Video Lesson 12
Mother-in-law	حَماتي/مَرت عَمِّي Hameiteh | mart 3ammeh Video Lesson 12

Father-in-law	عَمّي **3ammeh** Video Lesson 12

Friends

Friendship	صداقه **sadaa'a** <u>Video Lesson 24</u>
Friend	رفيئة/ رفيء/صديئة/صديء/صاحبتي/صاحِبي **rfee'a/rfee' | sadee'a/sadee' |** **saaHbeh/sahib** <u>Video Lesson 24</u>
Enemy	عَدوتي/عدُوّي **3adouweh/3adouw** <u>Video Lesson 24</u>
My best friend	هيّي رفيئَتي المُفَضَلَة/هوّي رفيئي المُفَضَل/هني رفئاتي المُفَضَلَين **hiyeh rfi'teh el** **moufaddaleh/howeh rfi'eh el** **moufaddal/henneh ref'aateh** **el moufaddaleen** <u>Video Lesson 24</u>
We go out	منُضـهَر **mnodhar** <u>Video Lesson 24</u>
We watch a movie	نِحنا منُحضَر فيلم **neHna mnoHdar film** <u>Video Lesson 24</u>

45

We have a drink	مِنُشرَب كاس **mneshrab keis** <u>Video Lesson 24</u>
We have fun	منتسلّى **mnetsalla** <u>Video Lesson 24</u>
We have dinner together	منتعشّى سوى **mnet3asha sawa** <u>Video Lesson 24</u>
We have coffee	مِنُشرَب قَهوه **mneshrab ahweh** <u>Video Lesson 24</u>
Let's do something	تَعي/تَعا/تعوا نَعمِل شي **ta3eh/ta3a/ta3o na3mil shi** <u>Video Lesson 24</u>
Have a drink with me	تَعي شرَبي/تَعا شراب/تعوا شربوا مَعي كاس **ta3eh shrabeh/ta3a shrab/ta3o shrabo ma3e keis** <u>Video Lesson 24</u>
Come over, we'll watch TV	تَعي/تَعا/تعوا لَعِندي مِنُحضَر تليفيزيون **ta3eh/ta3a/ta3o la 3andeh mnoHdar television** <u>Video Lesson 24</u>

| I'm inviting you to dinner | أنا عازمِتِك/عازمتَك/عازمتكُن على عَشا
3eizmetik/3eizmetak/3eizmet koun 3al 3asha
<u>Video Lesson 24</u> |

Love

Valentine's Day	عيد الحُب **3eed el Hobb** <u>Video Lesson 'Valentine'</u>
I love you	بحبِك/بحبَك/بحبكُن **bHebbik/bHebbak/bHebko un** <u>Video Lesson 'Valentine'</u>
I miss you	شتأتِلِك/شتأتلك/شتأتِلكن **shta'tellik/shta'tellak/shta'te llkoun** <u>Video Lesson 'Valentine'</u>
A kiss	بوسه **bawseh** <u>Video Lesson 'Valentine'</u>
Heart	ألب **aleb** <u>Video Lesson 'Valentine'</u>

Emotions

Emotion	إحساس/ شُعور eHseis | sho3our *Video Lesson 20*
Emotions	أحاسيس/ مَشاعِر aHasees | mashei3ir *Video Lesson 20*
Sadness	حِزن/ زَعَل Hezen | za3al *Video Lesson 20*
Depression	إحباط/ كآبه eHbaat | ka'abeh *Video Lesson 20*
Anger	تُعصيب to3seeb *Video Lesson 20*
Happiness	فَرَح/ سعاده faraH | sa3aadeh *Video Lesson 20*
Optimism	تَفاؤُل tafei'oul *Video Lesson 20*

Pessimism	تَشاؤُم **tashei'oum** <u>Video Lesson 20</u>
Orgasm	نشوه **nashweh** <u>Video Lesson 20</u>
Pride	فَخر **fakher** <u>Video Lesson 20</u>
Shyness	خَجَل **khajal** <u>Video Lesson 20</u>
Anxiety	ألأ **ala'** <u>Video Lesson 20</u>
I'm sad I want to cry	أنا زَعلاني/ أنا زَعلان بَدّي إبكي **ana ze3leineh/ze3lein baddeh ebkeh** <u>Video Lesson 20</u>
She is so depressed	هيّي كتير مُحبَطَة **hiyeh kteer moHbata** <u>Video Lesson 20</u>
He is so depressed	هوّي كتير مُحبَط **howeh kteer moHbat** <u>Video Lesson 20</u>

My friend is always angry	رفيئتي بِتضَلّ معَصبِي/ رفيئي بِضلّو معَصّب **rfee'teh betdalla m3assbeh/rfee'eh bidallo m3assab** <u>Video Lesson 20</u>
My cat is always happy to see me	بسَينتي دايما" بطُمبُسِت بَس تشوفني/ بسَيني دايما" بيمبُسِط بس يشوفني **bseynteh deyman btombosit bas tshoufneh/bsayneh deyman byombosit bas yshoufneh** <u>Video Lesson 20</u>
You should be optimistic	لازم تتفاءَل **lezim tetfei'al** <u>Video Lesson 20</u>
When I see a black cat I become pessimistic	لَمّا شوف بسيَن أسوَد بصير متشاءمة/متشاءَم **lamma shouf bseyn aswad bsir metshei'meh/metshei'am** <u>Video Lesson 20</u>
He/she is shy	هيّي بتسِتِحي/ هوّي بيسِتِحي **hiyeh btesteHeh/howeh byesteHeh** <u>Video Lesson 20</u>

She is always anxious	هيّي دايما" بتعتَل هَمّ **hiyeh deyman bto3tal hamm** Video Lesson 20

6 CHAPTER 5: CONJUGATION

To Have

I have	أنا عَندي **ana 3endeh** <u>Video Lesson 18</u>
You have	إنتِ عَندِك/ إنتَ عَندَك **enteh 3endik/enta 3endak** <u>Video Lesson 18</u>
He has	هوّي عَندو **howeh 3endo** <u>Video Lesson 18</u>
She has	هيّي عَندا **hiyeh 3enda** <u>Video Lesson 18</u>

We have	نِحنا عَنّا neHna 3enna <u>Video Lesson 18</u>
You have	إنتو عَندكُن ento 3endkoun <u>Video Lesson 18</u>
They have	هِنِّي عَندُن henneh 3endoun <u>Video Lesson 18</u>
I had	أنا كان عَندي ana kein 3endeh <u>Video Lesson 18</u>
You had	إنتِ كان عَندِك/ إنتَ كان عَندَك enteh kein 3endik/enta kein 3endak <u>Video Lesson 18</u>
He had	هُوّي كان عَندو howeh kein 3endo <u>Video Lesson 18</u>
She had	هِيِّي كان عَندا hiyeh kein 3enda <u>Video Lesson 18</u>
We had	نِحنا كان عَنّا neHna kein 3enna <u>Video Lesson 18</u>

You had	إنتو كان عَندكُن ento kein 3endkoun Video Lesson 18
They had	هِنّي كان عَندُن henneh kein 3endoun Video Lesson 18
I will have	أنا رَح يصير عَندي ana raH yseer 3endeh Video Lesson 18
You will have	إنتِ رح يصير عَندِك/إنتَ رح يصير عَندَك enteh raH yseer 3endik/enta raH yseer 3endak Video Lesson 18
He will have	هوّي رَح يصير عَندو howeh raH yseer 3endo Video Lesson 18
She will have	هيّي رَح يصير عَندا hiyeh raH yseer 3enda Video Lesson 18
We will have	نِحنا رَح يصير عَنّا neHna raH yseer 3enna Video Lesson 18
You will have	إنتو رَح يصير عَندكُن ento raH yseer 3endkoun Video Lesson 18

| They will have | هِنّي رَح يصير عَندُن
henneh raH yseer 3endoun
<u>Video Lesson 18</u> |

To Go

I'm going	أنا رايحة/ أنا رايح **ana rayHa/ana rayiH** <u>Video Lesson 13</u>
You are going	إنتِ رايحة/إنتَ رايح **enteh rayHa/enta rayiH** <u>Video Lesson 13</u>
He's going	هوّي رايح **howeh rayiH** <u>Video Lesson 13</u>
She's going	هيّي رايحة **hiyeh rayHa** <u>Video Lesson 13</u>
We are going	نِحنا رايحين **neHna rayHeen** <u>Video Lesson 13</u>
You are going	إنتو رايحين **ento rayHeen** <u>Video Lesson 13</u>
They are going	هِنِّي رايحين **henneh rayHeen** <u>Video Lesson 13</u>

I went	أنا رحت **ana reHet** Video Lesson 13
You went	إنتِ رحتي/ إنتَ رحت **enteh reHteh/enta reHet** Video Lesson 13
He went	هوّي راح **howeh raaH** Video Lesson 13
She went	هيّي راحت **hiyeh raaHit** Video Lesson 13
We went	نِحنا رحنا **neHna reHna** Video Lesson 13
You went	إنتو رحتوا **ento reHto** Video Lesson 13
They went	هنّي راحوا **henneh raaHo** Video Lesson 13
I will go	أنا رَح روح **ana raH rouH** Video Lesson 13

You will go	إنتِ رَح تروحي/ إنتَ رَح تروح enteh raH trouHeh/enta raH trouH Video Lesson 13
He will go	هوّي رَح يروح howeh raH yrouH Video Lesson 13
She will go	هيّي رَح تروح hiyeh raH trouH Video Lesson 13
We will go	نِحنا رَح نروح neHna raH nrouH Video Lesson 13
You will go	إنتو رَح تروحوا ento raH trouHo Video Lesson 13
They will go	هنّي رَح يروحوا henneh raH yrouHo Video Lesson 13

To Eat

I'm eating	أنا عَم باكُل ana 3am beikoul Video Lesson 16
You're eating	إنتِ عَم تاكلي/ إنتَ عَم تاكُل enteh 3am teikleh/enta 3am teikoul Video Lesson 16
He's eating	هوّي عَم ياكُل howeh 3am yeikoul Video Lesson 16
She's eating	هيّي عَم تاكُل hiyeh 3am teikoul Video Lesson 16
We're eating	نحنا عَم ناكل neHna 3am neikoul Video Lesson 16
You're eating	إنتو عَم تاكلوا ento 3am teiklo Video Lesson 16
They're eating	هنّي عَم ياكلوا henneh 3am yeiklo Video Lesson 16

I eat	أنا باكل **ana beikoul** <u>Video Lesson 16</u>
You eat	إنتِ بتاكلي/ إنتَ بتاكُل **enteh bteikleh/enta bteikoul** <u>Video Lesson 16</u>
He eats	هوّي بياكُل **howeh byeikoul** <u>Video Lesson 16</u>
She eats	هيّي بتاكُل **hiyeh btekoul** <u>Video Lesson 16</u>
We eat	نحنا مناكُل **neHna mneikoul** <u>Video Lesson 16</u>
You eat	إنتو بتاكلوا **ento bteiklo** <u>Video Lesson 16</u>
They eat	هِنّي بياكلوا **henneh byeiklo** <u>Video Lesson 16</u>
I ate	أنا أكَلت **ana akalet** <u>Video Lesson 16</u>

You ate	إنتِ أكَلتي/ إنتَ أكَلت enteh akalteh/enta akalet Video Lesson 16
He ate	هوّي أكَل howeh akal Video Lesson 16
She ate	هيّي أكَلِت hiyeh akalit Video Lesson 16
We ate	نحنا أكَلنا neHna akalna Video Lesson 16
You ate	إنتو أكلتوا ento akalto Video Lesson 16
They ate	هِنّي أكلوا henneh akalo Video Lesson 16
I will eat	أنا رَح آكل ana raH eikoul Video Lesson 16
You will eat	إنتِ رَح تاكلي/ إنتَ رَح تاكُل enteh raH teikleh/enta raH teikoul Video Lesson 16

He will eat	هوّي رَح ياكُل **howeh raH yeikoul** _Video Lesson 16_
She will eat	هيّي رَح تاكُل **hiyeh raH teikoul** _Video Lesson 16_
We will eat	نحنا رَح ناكُل **neHna raH neikoul** _Video Lesson 16_
You will eat	إنتو رَح تاكلوا **ento raH teiklo** _Video Lesson 16_
They will eat	هنّي رَح ياكلوا **henneh raH yeiklo** _Video Lesson 16_

To Draw

I draw	أنا بِرسُم **ana bersoum** <u>Video Lesson 19</u>
You draw	إنتِ بتِرسمي/ إنتَ بتِرسُم **enteh btersmeh/enta btersoum** <u>Video Lesson 19</u>
He draws	هوّي بيرسُم **howeh byersoum** <u>Video Lesson 19</u>
She draws	هيّي بتِرسُم **hiyeh btersoum** <u>Video Lesson 19</u>
We draw	نِحنا منرسُم **neHna mnersoum** <u>Video Lesson 19</u>
You draw	إنتو بتِرسموا **ento btersmo** <u>Video Lesson 19</u>
They draw	هِنّي بيرسموا **henneh byersmo** <u>Video Lesson 19</u>

I drew	أنا رَسَمت **ana rasamet** Video Lesson 19
You drew	إنتِ رَسَمتي/ إنتَ رَسَمت **enteh rasamteh/enta rasamet** Video Lesson 19
He drew	هُوّي رَسَم **howeh rasam** Video Lesson 19
She drew	هيّي رَسَمِت **hiyeh rasamit** Video Lesson 19
We drew	نِحنا رَسَمنا **neHna rasamna** Video Lesson 19
You drew	إنتو رَسَمتوا **ento rasamto** Video Lesson 19
They drew	هِنّي رَسَموا **henneh rasamo** Video Lesson 19
I used to draw	أنا كنت إرسُم **ana kenet ersoum** Video Lesson 19

You used to draw	إنتِ كنتِ تِرسمي/ إنتَ كِنت تِرسُم **enteh kenteh tersmeh/enta kenet tersoum** <u>Video Lesson 19</u>
He used to draw	هوّي كان يرسُم **howeh kein yersoum** <u>Video Lesson 19</u>
She used to draw	هيّي كانت تِرسُم **hiyeh keinit tersoum** <u>Video Lesson 19</u>
We used to draw	نِحنا كِنّا نِرسُم **neHna kenna nersoum** <u>Video Lesson 19</u>
You used to draw	إنتو كِنتوا ترسموا **ento kento tersmo** <u>Video Lesson 19</u>
They used to draw	هِنّي كانوا يرسموا **henneh keino yersmo** <u>Video Lesson 19</u>
I will draw	أنا رَح إرسم **ana raH ersoum** <u>Video Lesson 19</u>

You will draw	إنتِ رَح ترسمي/ أنتَ رح ترسُم enteh raH tersmeh/enta raH tersoum <u>Video Lesson 19</u>
He will draw	هوّي رَح يرسُم howeh raH yersoum <u>Video Lesson 19</u>
She will draw	هيّي رَح ترسُم hieyh raH tersoum <u>Video Lesson 19</u>
We will draw	نِحنا رَح نرسُم neHna raH nersoum <u>Video Lesson 19</u>
You will draw	إنتو رَح ترسموا ento raH tersmo <u>Video Lesson 19</u>
They will draw	هِنّي رَح يرسموا henneh raH yersmo <u>Video Lesson 19</u>

To Want

I want	أنا بَدّي **ana baddeh** <u>Video Lesson 6</u>
I want to eat	بَدّي آكُل **baddeh eikol** <u>Video Lesson 6</u>
I want to drink	بَدّي إشرب **baddeh eshrab** <u>Video Lesson 6</u>
I want to sleep	بَدّي نام **baddeh neim** <u>Video Lesson 6</u>
I want to work	بَدّي إشتِغِل **baddeh eshteghil** <u>Video Lesson 6</u>
I want to study	بَدّي إدرُس **baddeh edrous** <u>Video Lesson 6</u>
I want money	بَدّي مَصاري **baddeh masareh** <u>Video Lesson 6</u>

I want to dance	بَدِّي أرأص
	baddeh or'ous
	<u>Video Lesson 6</u>

7 CHAPTER 6: MISCELLANEOUS

Random Words and Sentences

Rice	رِز **rezz** Video Lesson 19
Button	زِر **zerr** Video Lesson 19
Horn	زَمّور **zammour** Video Lesson 19
Gun	فَرد **fared** Video Lesson 19

Fish	سَمَك **samak** Video Lesson 21
Guardian	حارِس **Haares** Video Lesson 21
Grass	حَشيش **hasheesh** Video Lesson 21
Improvisation	إرتِجال **ertijeil** Video Lesson 'Improvisation'
Flower	زهره **Zahra** Video Lesson 24
Rose syrup	شَراب الوَرد **sharaab el ward** Video Lesson '2nd Valentine'
I'm drinking coffee	أنا عَم بُشرَب قهوه **ana 3am beshrab ahweh** Video Lesson 'Improvisation'
I drink coffee everyday	بُشرَب قهوه كِل يوم **beshrab ahweh kel yom** Video Lesson 'Improvisation'

Today is Thursday and I'm going out later	اليوَم الخَميس،وبَعدين، أنا ضاهرة **lyom l khamees, w ba3dein, ana dahra** *Video Lesson 'Improvisation'*
It's September and it's becoming sad	نِحنا بأيلول والإشيا عَم بتصير حَزينِة **neHna b ayloul wel eshya 3am betseer Hazeeneh** *Video Lesson 'Improvisation'*
We are waiting for something	نِحنا ناطرين شي **neHna natreen shi** *Video Lesson 'Improvisation'*
This actress is improvising	هَيدي المَّسلي عم تِرتِجِل **haydeh el mmasleh 3am tertejil** *Video Lesson 'Improvisation'*
There are kids playing outside	في ولاد عَم تِلعَب بَرّا **fi wleid 3am tel3ab barra** *Video Lesson 'Improvisation'*
Today I ate "bazella w rezz"	اليوَم أكَلِت بَزيلّا ورزّ **lyom akalet bazella w rezz** *Video Lesson 'Improvisation'*

My favorite Lebanese dish is mjadra	أكلتي اللّبنانية المُفَضَّلة هيّي المجدَرا|أطيب أكلي عِندي هيّي المجدَرا **akelteh el lebneniyeh el moufaddaleh hiyeh el mjadra | atyab akleh 3endeh hiyeh el mjadra** Video Lesson 'Improvisation'
What are you doing this summer	شو عاَملي/عامِل/عاملين هَالصَيفيّه؟ **3aamleh/3aamil/3aamleen hal sayfiyeh** Video Lesson 23
Let's go to the beach	تَعي/تَعا/تعوا نروح عَلى بَحر **ta3eh/ta3a/ta3o nrouH 3al baHer** Video Lesson 23
I love to eat ice cream	بحب آكل بوظه **bHeb ekoul bouza** Video Lesson 23
Where can we go swim	وَين فينا نروح نِسبَح؟ **wein fina nrouH nesbaH** Video Lesson 23
Where's the nearest beach	وَين أَلرب بَحر؟ **wein a'rab baHer** Video Lesson 23

You should go to the beach before the summer ends	لازم تروحي/تروح/تروحوا عَلى البَحر أَبل ما تخلَص الصَيفيّه **lezim trouHeh/trouH/trouHo 3al baHer abel ma tokhlas l sayfiyeh** <u>Video Lesson 'Improvisation'</u>

8 CHAPTER 7: WORD PUZZLES

ACROSS

3 khareeta
5 3wayneit
7 beit
9 Hasheesh
10 tmeineh
11 aHad
13 bawseh
14 benneh
15 shmeil

DOWN

1 scarbeeneh
2 wleid
4 to3seeb
6 ala'
8 fostan
12 3an

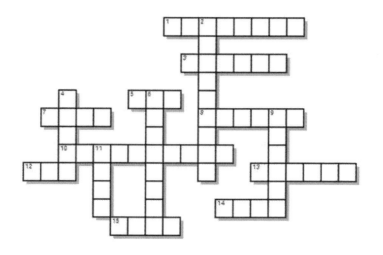

ACROSS

1 Haares
3 3ayleh
5 3ashra
7 enno
8 tanein
10 mat3am
12 bas
13 zerr
14 zammour
15 rmeideh

DOWN

2 she'a
4 amees
6 3afwan
9 khareef
11 sobbat

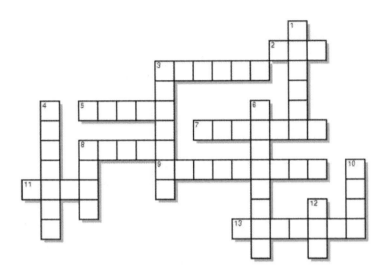

ACROSS

2 kif
3 rabee3
5 masareh
7 arkhas
8 tleiteh
9 shi
11 khamseh
13 addeh

DOWN

1 ahweh
3 khajal
4 sobeH
6 Hemmeim
8 henneh
10 samak
12 fared

ACROSS

2 zahra
4 khamees
7 wa
8 rezz
10 a'rab
11 lyom
13 sheiri3

DOWN

1 la'enno
2 arb3a
3 beshteghil
5 deghreh
6 marHaba
7 ba3dein
9 aleb
12 howeh

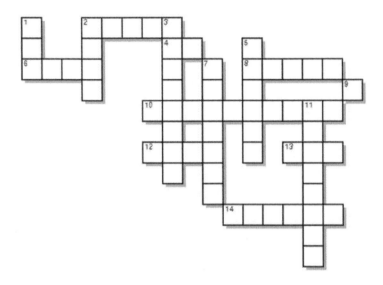

ACROSS

2 leil
4 3ala
6 doher
8 yameen
9 ana
10 sadaa'a
12 taree'
13 takhet
14 seif

DOWN

1 shames
2 tes3a
3 bukra
5 jem3a
7 taleita
11 bouza

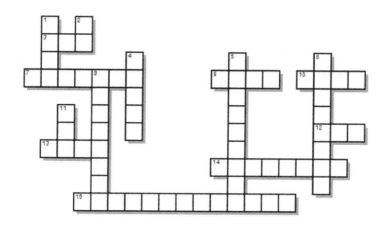

ACROSS

3 waHah
7 ahla w sahla
9 men
10 jem3a
12 hiyeh
13 ouda
14 sabet
15 ertijeil

DOWN

1 wardeh
2 neHna
4 sab3a
5 terwee'a
6 orb3a
8 tafei'oul
11 tnein

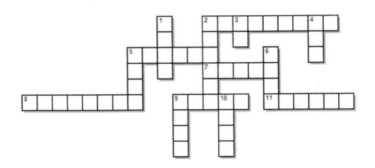

ACROSS

2 tashei'oum
5 sheteh
7 fakher
8 sou'aal
9 wein
11 nashweh

DOWN

1 zahreh
2 banafsajeh
3 fa
4 setteh
5 lamma
6 sefer
9 shou
10 ajaar

```
h  i  q  e  t  o  c  s  o  r
u  e  v  d  t  y  a  r  e  a
i  m  y  n  t  y  y  q  s  a
j  r  e  y  f  a  q  n  h  j
k  i  l  i  a  n  l  i  t  a
o  q  y  p  a  b  a  f  e  d
l  e  o  u  d  a  q  c  g  q
h  z  c  u  h  c  v  r  h  u
h  e  r  a  s  a  m  h  i  m
k  u  z  t  t  o  m  w  l  t
```

ajaar
alf
bayyeh
ento
eshteghil
kol
masareh
ouda
sayfiyeh

```
j  d  d  y  m  t  l  z  m  k
l  u  o  k  i  e  n  m  x  e
s  k  r  h  o  s  l  y  s  n
u  e  x  j  e  a  j  l  r  n
y  c  e  d  u  r  i  a  g  a
y  t  h  m  b  a  h  x  t  o
p  z  s  o  a  d  r  a  w  j
h  s  u  g  o  h  v  d  f  b
r  z  e  n  l  i  k  z  y  h
a  o  m  t  a  n  e  i  n  g
```

bouza
daraset
doher
kenna
khamees
mneikoul
mnodhar
tanein
ward

```
e b s l c j m x m w
i h c j u a m b q t
k z a a n o a a h l
o f r a k s k p a h
l c b z a a g i b e
h o e t v f l a e n
d e e t i m r n m n
g t n x v h b p a e
u m e r s q m i q h
j t h e b i e t k r
```

akalna
ana
eikol
eshrab
henneh
kteibeh
mbasatet
neikoul
scarbeeneh

```
h o p m j k y m g m
i e i t h h l p x u
t e r e g a i x k o
n e i e g l h r a s
v r r f e e z s m r
g t h s r h k q a e
l c n h o c g w s t
q v g q d u g z w b
h e y i h y m j l x
d n a t r e e n k h
```

btersoum
deghreh
hiyeh
khaleh
kheir
natreen
neim
samak
tersoum
zgheereh

Fill in the Blanks:

neHna halla' b _____ el rabee3, fi shames bas _____ kteer shob, w fi wleid _____ tel3ab barra.

marHaba, _____ eHjouz ouda zgheereh _____ takhet waHad, addeh lezim edfa3 iza _____ yeha la jem3a?

marHaba, baddeh rouH _____ Ashrafieh. ayya bus _____?

bl seif mn _____ 3al baHer. lezim trouH 3al baHer _____ ma tokhlas l sayfiyeh la'enno hala' neHna b ayloul wel ta'es _____ b seer sa'3a.

lyom l khamees, _____ 3am beshrab ahweh, w ba3dein, _____ 3al neideh

If you would like to download the solutions for the exercises, or you wish to print larger copies of the exercises please sign up at the following link for a PDF version of the puzzles and their solutions: **http://bit.ly/ExercisesPDF**
Just enter the link in the address bar of your internet browser and hit the Enter button.

9 CONCLUSION

If you enjoyed the book, I would be very glad if you leave an honest review on the Amazon page of the book. The reviews will help me know what works and what doesn't so I can fix them in this book, as well as in subsequent volumes.

To leave a review, please go to the Amazon page, scroll down to the end of the reviews, and click on "Write a customer review".

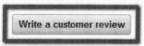

This   is   the   book's   Amazon   page: **http://bit.ly/Vol1amazon**

Thank you for reading my book, I hope you found it to be helpful. In case you have any questions about the Lebanese Dialect, fell free to post it on either my

Facebook page, or as a comment on my videos:

Facebook page:

Learn Lebanese Arabic

http://bit.ly/LearnLebaneseArabicFB

Youtube channel:

hiibanajem

http://bit.ly/hiibanajem1

And finally, if you would like to be notified of new videos, lessons and books please enter your email address here: http://bit.ly/FBolVIDoptin

ABOUT THE AUTHOR

Hiba Najem, has been teaching Lebanese Arabic online since 2011, and has fixed her method according to her students' needs and feedback. The social aspect of online teaching has helped her in developing her teaching into a very effective style.

Made in the USA
Columbia, SC
18 October 2024